Going Home

The Mystery of Animal Migration

By Marianne Berkes
Illustrated by Jennifer DiRubbio

Dawn Publications

For teachers everywhere who bring a sense of wonder to their classrooms.
And for my mentors, Barbara Lucas, Elinore Simon, and Sophia Visser, with love. — MB

To Matthew, Ryan, William, Emily, Christian and Paul:
Wherever life's journey takes you, my love will always be with you. — JDR

Special thanks to Debbie Fritz Quincy, Director of the Hobe Sound Nature Center for her review of this manuscript. Also thanks to the following for their help with the photos on the "Tips from the Author" page: June Parrilli and students at Hobe Sound Elementary School, Hobe Sound, Florida (Reader's Theater photo); The River Center in Jupiter, Florida (photo with turtle shell); and Lynn Gonzales, Children's Librarian, and Chris Hylton at "Planting Florida's Future" in Mt. Dora, Florida (photo with children and butterfly).

A Sharing Nature With Children Book

Library of Congress Cataloging-in-Publication Data
Berkes, Marianne Collins.
  Going home : the mystery of animal migration / by Marianne Berkes ; illustrated by Jennifer DiRubbio. -- 1st ed.
    p. cm.
  Summary: "A selection of animals that migrate by air, land and sea represents the variety and mystery of why and how animals migrate"--Provided by publisher.
  ISBN 978-1-58469-126-6 (hardback) -- ISBN 978-1-58469-127-3 (pbk.) 1. Animal migration--Juvenile literature. I. DiRubbio, Jennifer, ill. II. Title.
  QL754.B384 2010
  591.56'8--dc22

                    2009038568

Manufactured by Regent Publishing Services, Hong Kong,
Printed January, 2010, in ShenZhen, Guangdong, China
10 9 8 7 6 5 4 3 2 1
First Edition

Book design and production by Patty Arnold, Menagerie Design and Publishing

Dawn Publications

12402 Bitney Springs Road
Nevada City, CA 95959
530-274-7775
nature@dawnpub.com

Going home, going home,
We feel the urge to go.

It's time for us to travel on,

It's something we just know.

Many of us look for food,

Others find a mate.

And when the weather starts to change,

There is no time to wait.

Going home, going home,
Where I need to be.
Somehow I will paddle on,
Swimming endlessly.

From the ocean I will crawl,
Up onto the shore.
Laying eggs on a beach
Where I've been before.

Loggerhead turtles hatch from eggs that the mother buries on a sandy beach. They scurry into the ocean where they live for many years. When the female is ready to lay eggs, she usually swims back to the same beach where she was born.

Going home, going home,
Dancing in the sky.
Waking from our winter sleep,
It's time for us to fly.

We rested in our "family tree,"
Filling every space.
But now it's time to travel on
And find another place.

Monarch butterflies migrate south to keep warm when
winter approaches. They rest closely together in a semi-dormant
state, often on the very same trees their ancestors occupied the
year before. In spring, they fly north.

Going home, going home,
I can find my way.
Navigating toward the coast
Where I used to stay.

When it was cold I had to move.
I floated near the shore,
Until I found a warm lagoon
Where I could eat some more.

Manatees migrate as water temperatures change. If the water
is too cold, they will die. They often follow the same routes that
their parents did, chewing on vegetation along the way.

Going home, going home,
I feel the time is near.
I'm heading where I lay my eggs,
I do it every year.

I need to cross the wide blue sea
And then I'll eat my fill.
Rapidly I beat my wings
And use my slender bill.

Ruby-throated hummingbirds traveling between their winter and summer homes make an amazing non-stop crossing over the Gulf Mexico. When they reach land, they eagerly drink the sweet nectar from flowers for the energy they need to continue their journey.

Going home, going home,
Swimming wild and free,
To rivers that are cool and clear,
From the salty sea.

I leap! I splash! I charge upstream!
Swimming on and on.
I have to reach my place of birth—
It's where I go to spawn.

Pacific salmon lay eggs in fresh water streams.
The tiny fish swim toward the salty ocean,
where they live for a few years until fully grown.
Then they find the same river, and battle their
way upstream to their place of birth, to lay their
eggs (spawn).

Going home, going home,
Looking down below.
The season's here, the path is clear,
And we're all set to go.

Honking high in the sky
Flying in a "V."
We soar together in a flock,
Saving energy.

Canada geese fly together in a V formation which creates a current of air that makes it easier for them to fly. They "honk" loudly to each other—kind of like a buddy system. That way they keep track of each other without looking around.

Going home, going home,
Moving on our way,
Heading for some icy seas
From a nice warm bay.

Our babies swim beside us,
Staying close to shore,
Traveling up the coastline
Five thousand miles or more!

California gray whales spend the winter near
California and northern Mexico. In spring they
start the long journey to cold northern waters
where there is plenty to eat. The mothers stay
close to the coast to protect their babies from
killer whales.

Going home, going home,
Listen to the sounds!
Our thundering herd is setting out
To our vast calving grounds.

The journey spans two thousand miles,
But we were born to run!
We're on the treeless tundra now
And feel the Arctic sun.

Caribou gather in huge herds
in winter in evergreen forests,
where there is some protection
from the cold. In spring they
move northward to the tundra
to feed on lichens and other
low-growing plants and to give
birth to their young.

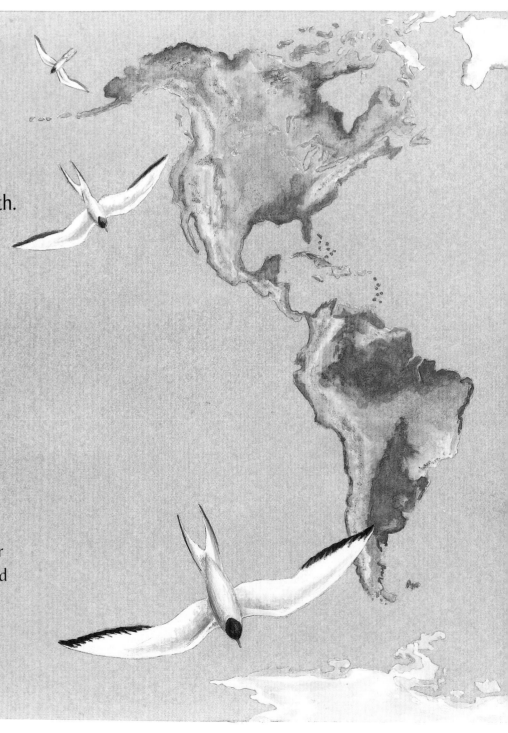

Going home, going home,
I have the longest way.
I travel all around the globe
To see the light of day!

I'm always moving north and south.
I really love to fly.
I nest up in the Arctic,
And dive for food supply.

The **Arctic tern** is the world's champion
migrator. It travels over 20,000 miles every year
to live in almost constant sunshine. In June and
July it enjoys almost constant sunshine in the
Arctic summer; in December and January it
enjoys almost constant sunshine in the
Antarctic summer.

Going home, going home,
I never use the sky.
I flap my wings in water—
And that is how I "fly!"

My mate will keep our baby warm
While I feed in the sea.
And then I'll waddle miles on ice
To find my family.

Emperor penguins "fly" through the water, propelled by their flippers. They live mostly in water, but in winter they migrate inland onto ice, where the female lays a single egg. Then she goes back to the ocean to feed, while the egg is kept warm by the male.

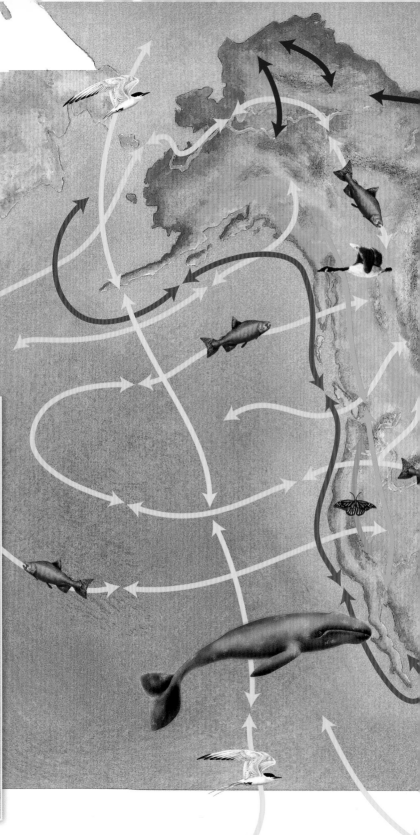

Going home, going home,
By land, by sky, by sea.
Our journey back from "here" to "there"
Is still a mystery.

We have to move from place to place—
You know the reasons now.
Our genius is to know the way,
And yours to wonder, "HOW"?

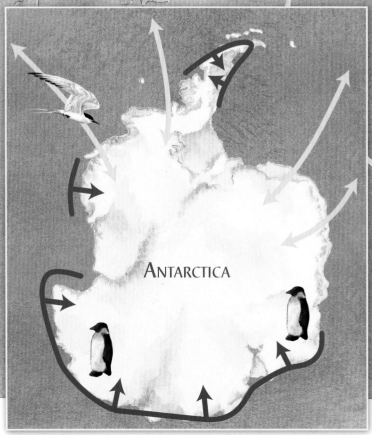

ANTARCTICA

(NOT TO SCALE)

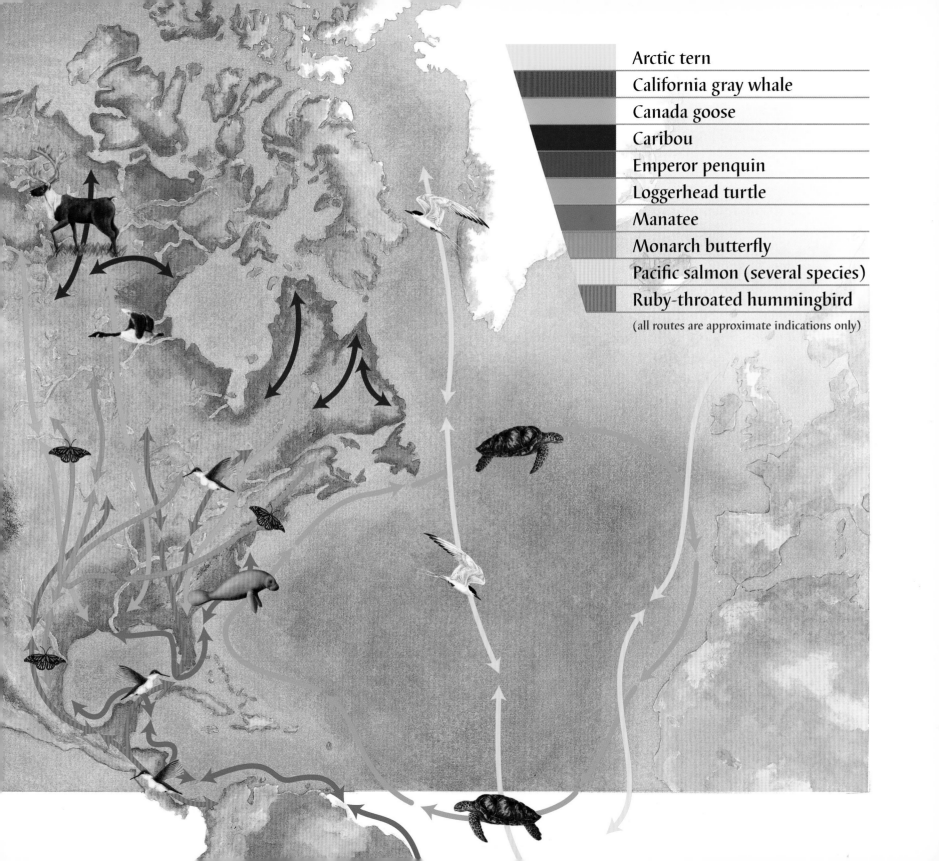

Arctic tern
California gray whale
Canada goose
Caribou
Emperor penquin
Loggerhead turtle
Manatee
Monarch butterfly
Pacific salmon (several species)
Ruby-throated hummingbird

(all routes are approximate indications only)

The Mystery of Migration

The rhyming verses you read in this story were told in the voice of the animals themselves. Of course they don't talk—that is fiction. But their adventures and their migration routes are amazingly real—that is non-fiction. Taken together, this kind of book is called "creative non-fiction."

Migration is usually a seasonal, lengthy journey from one place to another. Migrators do this to stay warm, raise their young, and find plenty of food and water. Sometimes it might take a lifetime to complete, such as for the Pacific salmon. Occasionally it may take several lifetimes for a species to complete, as in the case of the monarch butterfly.

Often these animals find their way instinctively to the very same spot, finding the same river or beach or tree, even though they had never been there before except when they were born. In the case of butterflies, only their ancestors had been there before!

Imagine yourself being one of these animals. Why would you feel the urge to migrate? What would it take to travel on such long and dangerous journeys? What obstacles might you face? How would you find your way? These creatures hardly ever wander off course. Unlike humans, animals don't have maps or other navigational devices such as compasses or satellite systems! Could it be that they have "navigational devices" in their brains? Some scientists think so, but nobody is sure. Maybe you will be a scientist who solves the mystery or a writer who tells the real story.

How to Learn More about the Animals

Books:

All About Manatees by Jim Arnosky (Scholastic, 2008)

Animals That Migrate by Carmen Bredeson (Franklin Watts, 2001)

It's a Hummingbird's Life by Irene Kelly (Holiday House, 2003)

A Monarch Butterfly's Life by John Himmelman (Children's Press, 2000)

National Geographic Complete Birds of North America by Jonathan Alderfer (National Geographic, 2005)

Ocean Commotion: Sea Turtles by Janeen Mason (Pelican, 2007)

One Tiny Turtle by Nicola Davis, (Candlewick Press, 2005)

Salmon Stream by Carol Reed-Jones (Dawn, 2000)

What is Migration? by John Crossingham and Bobbie Kalman (Crabtree, 2001)

Websites:

http://www.audubon.org
http://www.learner.org/jnorth/
http://bna.birds.cornell.edu/bna/
http://www.sciencemadesimple.com/animals
http://www.salmonnation.com/fish/meet_species.html
http://www.monarchwatch.org
http://www.monarchlab.umn.edu
http://www.enchantedlearning.com/coloring/migrate
http://www.savethemanatee.org/
http://www.pbs.org/kqed/oceanadventures/educators/whales

Movies:

DVD: "March of the Penguins" narrated by Morgan Freeman
DVD: "Winged Migration" narrated by Jacques Perrin

About the Migrating Animals

Loggerhead turtles live in the Atlantic, Pacific, and Indian Oceans. The babies are about two inches long when they plunge into the ocean immediately after hatching. If they hatch on a North Atlantic beach, they will float into the North Atlantic Gyre, a giant current that circles clockwise. For twenty years or more they follow the gyre for about 8,000 miles. After mating, a female heads for the same beach where she hatched, thousands of miles away. There she digs a nest, lays her eggs, and then swims back to the ocean. Male loggerheads never return.

Monarch butterflies fly thousands of miles every autumn to spend the winter in Mexico or California. Monarchs east of the Rocky Mountains go to Mexico; those west of the Rockies go to California. They go to the same areas, often to the same trees as their ancestors did, roosting in a semi-dormant state. In spring they fly north and lay eggs on milkweed plants. Then they die. Their offspring continue the journey, lay more eggs, and another generation begins. Several generations later, when autumn arrives, the cycle starts all over again. Remarkably, they have no individual memory of their destination; rather it is the great grandchildren, or great-great grandchildren or great-great-great grandchildren, who will find the same warm spot to roost next winter.

Manatees migrate seasonally when water temperatures change. In summer months the West Indian manatees, also called the Florida manatees, may travel along the Atlantic shoreline as far north as Virginia; but when the water cools to below 70 degrees, they must move to warmer water. Sometimes manatees swim up rivers. They swim slowly, only two to six miles per hour. Manatees are also called "sea cows" because they chew on lots of vegetation. Similar species of manatees live near the coasts of Africa, Australia, Indonesia, and the east coast of South America.

Ruby-throated hummingbirds are tiny but strong birds that live in the eastern United States and Canada in summer and in Mexico and Central America in winter. The Gulf of Mexico is a huge obstacle for them. Some of them travel around the west side of the Gulf, through Texas and Mexico. Others fly directly between Florida and Mexico, making an amazing 500 mile non-stop crossing, beating their wings 75 times every second and attaining speeds of 30 miles per hour. When they arrive on land, they are hungry and exhausted, and immediately sip nectar from flowers. Unlike most birds, a hummingbird can hover in mid-air or fly backwards, its tiny wings a blur of motion.

Pacific salmon include several species, all of which lay eggs in the fresh water of streams. When the newly hatched fish are about an inch long, they are called "fry" and they eat tiny insects and plants. Some species start to migrate to the ocean almost immediately. Others may stay in streams and rivers for a year or more. They swim far into the ocean for up to five years. Then they head home to the very same river and tributary of their birth, swimming upstream sometimes as much as a thousand miles and climbing as much as 7,000 feet above sea level.

Canada geese mate for life. They breed at their summer home in Canada and the northern United States. Usually the female returns to the same area where her parents nested. In winter, the family seeks warmer climates. Although some winter over in southern Canada, most migrate to the mid and southern United States. The "V" flight formation saves energy by creating a current of air that makes it easier for geese toward the back of the "V" to fly. They "honk" to each other—a buddy system—so they can keep track of each other and avoid crashing into each other. The Canada goose is the most familiar and widespread goose in North America. It can be found in wetlands from the tundra to the Gulf coast. Many of them live in the Great Lakes region.

California gray whales have the longest migration route of any mammal—a 10,000 to 14,000 mile round trip. In winter, whales give birth in warm lagoons near Mexico. In spring, they head north, traveling for two to three months along the Pacific coast. To breathe they come to the water's surface and blow through their blowholes, forming a plume of mist and spray that can be seen from far away. During summer they eat tons of plankton and fish in the cold water of the Bering Sea. Their bodies store the energy from this food as a thick layer of blubber under the skin, which also keeps them warm. When they go south for the winter, they eat very little, primarily living off energy stored in their blubber.

Caribou travel in herds of up to 100,000 animals and are almost always on the move. They sometimes run nearly 50 miles per hour and travel over 1,000 miles in their migrations, using the same routes every year. They can be heard from a distance because their legs make a loud clicking sound when they run. In spring they move north to the tundra where they give birth to their young. In fall, herds move south to evergreen forests where they have more protection from the cold and where there is better food supply. Caribou dig deeply into the snow to eat lichens and other low-growing plants. Large herds also live in Scandinavia and Siberia, where they are called reindeer.

The **Arctic tern** is the champion long-distance traveler of the animal world. The tern may also be the world's most dedicated sunbather! They travel over 20,000 miles each year, flying over the ocean almost all the time, so that they can live in almost constant daylight. During the Arctic summer, when the North Pole is tilted toward the sun, the sun shines almost all the time. This is when the terns breed and nest. The Arctic offers plenty of food— terns plunge-dive from the air to catch fish. When the days grow shorter, they fly to Antarctica, where summer is just starting. As with the Arctic summer, the sun shines almost all the time during the Antarctic summer.

Emperor penguins are the largest of 17 species of penguins. They live only in the Antarctic, not the Arctic. In summer they live and feed far out into the ocean. Their wings are shaped like flippers so they "fly" underwater. They have shiny, waterproof feathers well adapted to icy environments that help keep their skin dry. They pick winter—the coldest time of the year in the coldest place on Earth—to raise their young! Each fall they walk inland 30 to 70 miles over ice to breeding sites. After the female lays a single egg, the male incubates it for about 70 days, balancing it on his feet under a warm flap of skin. Meanwhile the female waddles back to the ocean to eat, and then finds her way back to feed her chick.

Tips from the Author

I hope you will discover something new and exciting each time you read my book. Going Home, The Mystery of Animal Migration offers many opportunities for extended activities. Here are a few ideas.

FIND THEIR ROUTE

Go to www.dawnpub.com and click on "Educator Tools." Then look for the cover of this book. There you will be able to download the map on pages 25-26 without the animals' migration routes. Can you track their migrations? (Note: Primary Grade Teachers may want to put in dotted lines to give their students a head start.)

Loggerhead turtle: If migrating to a beach in the U.S., they would swim from somewhere in the North Atlantic Ocean to beaches from Virginia to Florida or on the Gulf coast west to Texas. The largest numbers go to south Florida.

Monarch butterfly: between Mexico and almost anywhere in the U.S. or Canada except the far north.

Manatee: between rivers or lagoons in Florida and coastal waters in the Atlantic as far north as Virginia.

Ruby-throated hummingbird: between Central America and anywhere on the east coast or Midwest, including southern Canada.

California gray whale: between Baja California, Mexico and the Bering Sea.

Canada goose: between southern U.S. and northern U.S. and Canada.

Pacific salmon: between somewhere in the North Pacific Ocean and a river or stream on the west coast of the U.S. or Canada.

Caribou: between north central Alaska and Canada and the tundra near the Arctic coast.

Emperor penguin: between coastal Antarctica and nesting grounds about 50 miles inland.

Arctic tern: between Antarctica and the Arctic, usually flying over the oceans.

DRAW YOUR OWN MAP

Draw your own map and plot other animals that migrate. See the "enchanted learning" website for a list of migrating animals.

READER'S THEATER

Teachers can use this book for a reader's theater to develop fluency and enhance comprehension. Ask students to choose one of the animals and pretend they are that animal. Think about how each animal might stand or move, and how to read the verse. For example, read manatee slowly and hummingbird quickly. Students can recite the first and last verse of this story in unison. As background music, you may want to use Antonin Dvorak's Symphony No. 9 (the "New World" symphony). The tune of the largo movement fits the words to "Going Home." For more information on reader's theater see: http://www.readwritethink.org/lessons/lesson_view.asp?id=172

CONSTRUCT AN ATTRIBUTE CHART

Draw a grid of facts about the migrating animals in this book. On the top horizontal sections of the grid enter category headings such as how the animal traveled (land, air or sea), reason for travel, length of trip or any other facts students have gathered from the book. On the left-hand section of the grid write the names of the ten migrating animals. Fill in the gird spaces for each animal.

BOOKMARKS

You can download reproducible bookmarks of the animals in this book. Click on the "Educator Tools" button at www.dawnpub.com.

WHO AM I?

Ask students to choose one of the creatures in this book and write two sentences describing the animal, but not mentioning which one it is. For example: I have the longest migration route of any mammal in the world. I breathe air through a blowhole. Who am I?

WRITE YOUR OWN STORY

Many animals migrate and offer wonderful opportunities for creative writing. Choose an animal not mentioned in this book, find out about it, then write about it. I wrote "The Wonder of It All" as an example. Your character will have its own unique story and you can tell it in the way you like best. Have fun with your own creation about an animal that is "going home." I would love to hear from teachers and parents on ways you have used this book. www.MarianneBerkes.com

THE WONDER OF IT ALL

(An example of creative non-fiction by Marianne Berkes)

On a moonlit beach, a baby sea turtle frantically climbed out of a nest filled with broken eggshells and down a sandy slope toward the sea. She got out just before a creature with a black mask, searching for an evening meal, started slurping up the egg yolks that the newborns had left behind.

She scrambled to the water's edge with her many siblings. Hungry crabs crawled after some of the hatchlings, while others were devoured by squawking sea gulls, but luckily the loggerhead turtle in this story made it into the ocean.

She splashed in a frenzy for several days in an ocean swarming with sharks, bluefish, and other hungry predators. Finally she found a huge patch of drifting sargasso seaweed and there she hid. She found tiny shrimp and other seafood in the floating camouflage and she grew bigger and stronger. After a while the seaweed didn't hide her anymore. She was heavier than most humans—over 250 pounds and almost 3 feet long. It was time to explore!

Now a young adult, the loggerhead turtle floated over colorful coral reefs filled with an abundance of sea life. She paddled thousands of miles in the wide and often treacherous Atlantic Ocean, past the Azore Islands, and past the Canary Islands, in a vast clockwise circle. She wandered in the sea for many years, finding plenty of crabs and mollusks to eat. But she was always on the lookout for sharks and other large fish that would devour her.

One day, far out in the Atlantic, she mated with a male loggerhead. Soon, she knew, it would be time to swim back to the beach of her birth twenty years ago. How would she find her way? Somehow she knew it was a journey she had to make.

Instinctively this great "nomad of the sea" found her beach. Graceful and buoyant in water, she now dragged herself ashore with her flippers. Crawling up the beach, she rotated her bulky body to move the sand.

She dug a deep chamber and dropped over a hundred ping-pong-ball-shaped eggs into her nest. Then with her rear flippers she pushed sand over the chamber and packed the sand to cover the eggs. With her front flippers she threw sand in all directions to disguise the nest.

When her work was done, Mama Loggerhead pulled her heavy body around and slowly crawled down to the water's edge. Then, in the moonlight, she paddled out to the welcoming arms of the sea.

Marianne Berkes has spent much of her life as a teacher, children's theater director, and children's librarian. She knows how much children enjoy "interactive" stories and is the author of eight entertaining and educational picture books that make a child's learning relevant. Reading, music, and theater have been a constant in Marianne's life. Her books are also inspired by her love of nature. She hopes to open kids' eyes to the magic found in our natural world. Marianne now writes full time. She also visits schools and presents at conferences. She is an energetic presenter who believes that "hands on" learning is fun. Her website is www.MarianneBerkes.com.

Jennifer DiRubbio is both a passionate artist and an avid environmentalist. She has been active as an artist for several organizations that promote nature and a healthy planet. Jennifer graduated with a BFA from Pratt Institute in 1992. She keeps her home and studio in Merrick, New York, as "green" and environmentally sound as possible, where her husband and two young children also work and play.

AWARD-WINNING BOOKS BY MARIANNE BERKES

Over in the Ocean: In a Coral Reef, illustrated by Jeanette Canyon — Illustrated in vivid polymer clay, this book portrays a delightful community of sea creatures.

Over in the Jungle: A Rainforest Rhyme, illustrated by Jeanette Canyon — As with "Ocean," this book captures a rain forest teeming with remarkable creatures.

Over in the Arctic: Where the Cold Winds Blow, illustrated by Jill Dubin — In the Arctic, the snow goose "honks" and the wolf "howls"—and so will children, joyfully. Illustrations are in cut paper.

Going Around the Sun: Some Planetary Fun, illustrated by Janeen Mason — Our Earth is part of a fascinating planetary family: eight planets and an odd bunch of solar system "cousins." Illustrations use melted crayon, in part.

Seashells by the Seashore, illustrated by Robert Noreika — Kids discover, identify, and count twelve beautiful shells to give Grandma for her birthday.

AWARD-WINNING BOOKS ILLUSTRATED BY JENNIFER DIRUBBIO

Under One Rock: Bugs, Slugs and Other Ughs, by Anthony D. Fredericks. A whole community of creatures lives under rocks. No child will be able to resist taking a peek after reading this.

In One Tidepool: Crabs, Snails and Salty Tails, by Anthony D. Fredericks. Have you ever ventured to the edge of the sea and peered into a tidepool? A colorful community of creatures lives there!

Around One Cactus: Owls, Bats and Leaping Rats, by Anthony D. Fredericks. A saguaro cactus may look lonely, standing in the dry, dry desert—but it is a haven for creatures, both cute and creepy!

Near One Cattail: Turtles, Logs and Leaping Frogs, by Anthony D. Fredericks. What creatures live in a bog-boggy place? Many—and they swim, soar and crawl!

On One Flower: Butterflies, Ticks and a Few More Icks, by Anthony D. Fredericks. A goldenrod flower is a "minibeast park," have you noticed? Take a closer look.

Dawn Publications is dedicated to inspiring in children a deeper understanding and appreciation for all life on Earth. To review our titles or to order, please visit us at www.dawnpub.com, or call 800-545-7475.